THE
DASH

WHAT WILL YOUR DASH SAY ABOUT YOU?

ELOY HUERTA

ISBN-13: 978-1-7345273-5-3
Printed in the United States of America

RevMedia Publishing
PO BOX 5172
Kingwood, TX 77325

A publishing division of Revelation Ministries
www.revmediapublishing.com

1 2 3 4 5 6 7 8 9 10 11 21 20 19 18 17 16 15 14

Here's what people are saying about "*The DASH*" and Eloy Huerta

Pastor Eloy's book "*The DASH*" had a major impact on my life. While reading I felt as if Eloy was having a conversation with me. The words in each chapter were so relatable and relevant. I highly recommend this book!

—Jared Miller
Author, Speaker and Leadership Coach, Jared Miller Ministries

Five stars! Loved it! Completely genuine, honest and humbling.

Eloy Huerta is passionate and genuine about God, family and people as he touches on real life situations. This book will be one that makes you think about how you want your legacy to read.

—Lisa Brush
Founder of FAITHMAT & Faith Moves Womens Ministry, wife and mother

I enjoyed the chapter about The Tithe. I liked how Eloy explained it. Even though I am a tither it was explained so simple for any person to understand.

—Travis Waldrep
Husband

Ever read a book and couldn't put it down?
Well, here's another one! Eloy sums it all up in a direct and to-the-point message. He was able to open my eyes to areas of my life I've been dismissing. I've got some work to do. Thank you Eloy, for taking the time to write this book.

—Estaban Garcia
Father and husband

Easy read, couldn't put it down.
I especially liked the chapter about Tithing. It does a good job of explaining God's blessing associated with cheerful giving without placing the reader under the "Law" of tithing.

—Carl Bowman
Husband, father and grandfather

What will your life's legacy be?
Eloy ministers to mostly men, but I really enjoyed reading this book. Eloy explains in detail tough topics which was really good. I loved it and it's a must read for men!

Norma Ortiz
Womens counselor, wife, mother and grandmother

WOW! I needed this!
What a refreshing reminder to me about being a Man of God. Your book spoke to me about leaving a Legacy in Christ. Thanks Eloy.

—Pastor Aaron Thomas
Founder and Director of P.E.A.C.E Outreach Ministry

Dedication

I would like to dedicate this book to Pastor Walter Hallam. Pastor Hallam has been a great role model to so many men throughout the years. He was my pastor for over a decade and while under his teaching and guidance I was able to become the husband, father and man of God that God desires me to be.

Also, I would like to recognize my father Ernesto Huerta. Even though we were not raised in a religious home, my dad taught me about family, hard work and that in life, your name matters.

CONTENTS

INTRODUCTION

I would like for you to be honest with yourself for a moment. If you were to give yourself a grade as a husband what grade would that be? _____ . How about as a father? _____ . Let's take it a little farther. How about as a Man of God? _____ . I left some lines there so you could write down an honest grade and hopefully after reading this book you will see the change in you. Better yet maybe your wife and kids will notice the difference.

Let me tell you my grades so you don't get discouraged. As a husband, I was a D. As a father, maybe a <u>C+</u> or <u>B-</u>, and as a Man of God a big fat <u>F</u>.

You see, at one time I was not very good. There were some things that needed to be changed in me. It was always about me, me and me. I know none of you reading this book are like that.

I titled this book *The DASH* because the dash between your birth year and the day that you leave this earth will determine the kind of legacy that you leave with those that matter the most.

Some of you might say that I am not married or I don't have any children so this does not pertain to me. Oh my friend but it does. Are you a Man of God? Are you an uncle helping that sister raise those kids? Whether you know it or not they are watching you.

I would like for you to say a simple prayer before reading this book. Say this out loud.

Jesus help me to see the things that I need to change in me. Help me grow in every area, as a husband, father, uncle, mentor, and step-father but especially as a man of God. In Jesus name, Amen. I am in agreement with you and proud of you for stepping up.

Blessings to you,

—*Eloy Huerta*

CHAPTER 1

What Legacy are you Leaving?

Imentioned earlier about the title being *The Dash*. It could have easily been titled "What Legacy are you Leaving". Because, whether you know it or not you are leaving a legacy.

Many years ago I was in Pasadena, Texas. I was at the hospital visiting someone and I was told that a co-worker's mother had passed away. I decided to look at the obituary for the funeral home because they also lived in Pasadena and I was hoping to stop by and express my condolences. I was not able to locate the funeral home and later I was able to pay my respects to my co-worker. How many of you know that the Lord orders our steps?

The Lord had a plan for me to search the obituary. After searching several pages, I noticed one obituary that took almost 1/3 of the page. I read this obituary several times because I was in such AWE of the legacy that this man left. The obituary was written by his wife and children. This man had not even reached 50 years of age. I would have figured that he was older.

Most of you know that an obituary is usually a few lines and basically says something like this: Joe died yesterday. Funeral is tomorrow at 3:00 at St. Mary's.

I continued reading and the Lord said "What would your legacy be, Eloy"? I started thinking where do I stand with God? What would my wife say about me if I died? I started thinking what about my children. What legacy would I leave for them?

In that moment I started to think of messages that my pastor had ministered on like: Your name is important or are you training up your children in the way they should go? So, as I thought more and more about it, I started to ask myself what I might need to change within myself. The Lord said that He wanted me to teach more about the legacy we as men would be leaving. So, I started to teach more about it at our next meeting and the response was incredible. Men wanted to hear more about it and their wives would tell me things like, "I don't know what you told my husband, but I can see a difference in him lately and it is for the better."

Men would ask me after the meetings what books they should read to keep improving. A nerve was struck or shall I say God struck a nerve. Men would call me and ask questions about relationships, kids or to just say how they have enjoyed the truth about needing to change.

I have heard story after story about just a simple question like "What grade would you give yourself as a husband, father or man of God." It got them thinking. Then I would ask them "What grade would your wife give you?" "What about your kids?" "Ok, how about God?" You could hear a pin drop when I asked that.

You see, we can give ourselves a grade and walk away knowing that we are not truthful. But, when we ask ourselves, "What grade would my family give me?", "What would God say about me?" Then we have to look at the whole picture and say, "I wonder what the grade would be?" I want to ask you a question. Are you leaving a mark or a scar with your wife and kids? We would like to think that everything is ok, but if we really think about it, we all have some type of issue.

Some of us are leaving scars everywhere we go. The trails of hurt, tears, deception and lies. When will you say "enough is enough?" It is time for a change. Leave a mark that you can be proud of, as well as your wife and children. When it is all said and done, God can look at you and say, "Well done good and faithful servant. You blessed and prospered the family that I gave you."

CHAPTER 2

Moving Forward From The Past

How many times have you heard or maybe even said the following: "You just don't know what I have been through". I have heard it more than I can count. In the Bible you will see story after story of what God's people had been through. The best part is that you and I are able to see how God got them through every situation. They were able to move forward.

In the book of Joshua 1: 1-18 you will read that Moses has died and it is Joshua's job to move the Israelites across the Jordan River. Just like us, Joshua could have said "Wait God, I am not ready". Joshua could have said "Give me more time" or better yet "God, how about using Caleb"? What God had done was prepared Joshua "for such a time as this". Just like God has prepared you to step up.

One thing that you have to realize is that God has been preparing you through all these situations. Those past failures, past sins and even those past hurts will help you become the Man of God that He desires you to be. Throughout that first chapter in the book of Joshua. God tells Joshua "I will never leave you nor forsake you". God also tells Joshua, if you follow what I say in leading the people over the Jordan River I will be with you.

Listen, the best way to move forward is to repent and forgive those that have hurt you as well as forgiving yourself. In life we will always have people or situations that stop us in our tracks, so to speak. I heard a man say that you cannot unscramble a scrambled egg. You have to move forward.

If you want to live a healthy spiritual life, ask the Lord to help you daily. It is not going to happen overnight. In the book of Matthew 18: 21-22 Jesus tells Peter to forgive people seventy times seven. That's four hundred and ninety times to forgive people per day. What I believe the Lord is trying to say is that by the time you go on to forgive after about the 5th or 6th time you will be able to move on. By that time it will hardly cross our mind anymore. The Lord wants you to walk in forgiveness constantly. If you remember it again, start to forgive again.

We cannot always look at those people that are getting on our nerves as a bad thing. Have you ever looked at it as maybe the Lord sent them so you can pray more or maybe so you can have more patience? Our first way to think seems to always be, "Lord why me"? Or "Lord get rid of them". We should look at this situation that this is getting me closer to God by being in constant prayer? Maybe, you should say, "Lord thank you for sending those people my way". It is helping me walk in peace, love and joy daily. Maybe, The Lord is preparing you for your next situation.

I would like to tell you a situation that I had many years ago. Little did I know that God was preparing me, I can honestly say that my first reaction was "Why me Lord"? I worked with a guy that always knew how to push my buttons and not for the better. I was a young Christian and I tried to be Christ- like but like most young Christians we don't always react like we should. I know that I am probably not the only one to ever go through this. I really and truly thought that my heart was right and my reactions were not wrong. God told me one day to ask this man to forgive me for everything that I had done to him. I said, "God are you seeing everything this man has done to me"? "You want me to apologize"? "I said I am not doing it God".

I waited at least two weeks and God, knowing the answer, says to me, "Have you asked him to forgive you yet"? You see my first reaction was this man should apologize to me. God has plans that we do not see because He is all knowing. God knows my future. He knew that my heart was hurting. God knew the pain that I was going through daily. God knew that I had to move forward. So, I asked this man to step into the office and I asked him if he would forgive me for everything that I had done to him. To my surprise he said, "That is the dumbest thing that I have ever heard". The Lord spoke to my heart instantly and said, "You have done your part. Don't say anything else". Just then it felt like a ton of bricks just lifted off my shoulders. My heart was right and I could walk away with a peace that I never had before. I just smiled and said, "Sir, I have done my part" and he walked away madder than a hornet. Now when faced with the same situation I can spot those type of people from a mile away.

God is always preparing us. I am able to walk with peace and when people ask me, "How do you do it"? I just say God prepared me years ago and I think back to all the things that I had to endure to move forward. If I would not have changed my way of thinking or how I respond to the negative, then I probably would not be leaving *The Dash* that I am leaving. When will you move forward and leave *The Dash* that you desire to leave?

CHAPTER 3

What Does She Really Want?

I heard a joke about a man that was walking along the California Coast. As he was walking, he found a bottle. As he opened it, a Genie popped out. The Genie says "You have one wish". The man thought about it for a minute and says, "I have always wanted to travel to Hawaii but I am afraid to fly. I would like a highway to go from California to Hawaii." The Genie says, "that is too difficult. Do you know how much cement and foundation that it would take from here to Hawaii? It is impossible! I will grant you a different wish." The man thinks about it and says, "I have always wanted to understand women. How they think, and what they want. That has always been a desire of mine". The Genie looks at him and says "do you want a two lane highway or four lane"?

I know this is a joke but most of us men have a difficult time trying to understand our wives. We think we have them figured out then out of nowhere they start crying. I have been married over thirty years and I will try to help you the best that I can. As I was writing the titles of each chapter of this book as The Lord was giving them to me, I said "Lord, I am going to need your help with this one".

One of the things we have to understand is that women are wired different. Some men do not think of the future like women do. We get paid and want to go spend the money right away. A woman will look at a paycheck and say," How long can this last? We need groceries, we need to pay the house note or we need to have enough until next paycheck".

When a young lady marries a young man, he promises her a house, a future family and of course plenty of everything. Little did she know that the house they were going to live in was his parents' house? And they are still in it. She starts to think, "What did I get myself into?"

A woman wants and desires her husband to have a vision. She wants to know. "Where are you taking me? Can I have a future with this man? How does he treat his mom? Is he a momma's boy? Does he show her respect? Does he hug his mom? Does he yell at his mom? How is he around his nephews and nieces? Does he have patience? Is this what I want in my life"?

She also looks at this man and says things like, "Does he desire a relationship with God? Does he seek council from wise men when there is a problem, or does he go to foolish people? People that will tell him what he wants to hear? I have a question for you sir, Are you doing these things? You see she is watching you.

I am going to ask you to picture a see-saw. Maybe you know it as a teeter-totter. You are sitting on one side and she is on the other side. If the side you are sitting on is on the ground more often, then it is more about you.

In any marriage you will always have ups and downs. But, you have to understand that there is give-and-take for a marriage to work.

I want to share a true story about a friend that wanted to be on a deer lease. Because it would cost several thousand dollars he decided to take his wife and show her where the deer lease was and why they would be spending so much money. After showing her around the place they decided to stop at the local burger joint. As they ordered she requested extra cheese on the burger. He said, No way! "Do you know how much that extra piece of cheese cost"? She looked back at him and said "How much is that deer lease again"? He quickly said to the lady taking the order, "Extra cheese please".

She wants to be shown that she matters not just told that she matters. She wants to be looked at like when you were dating. When was the last time you bought her flowers and it was not your anniversary or Valentine's Day? When was the last time you treated her like your wife and not like one of the guys, until it's time for some hanky panky? She does not want to be used and abused.

You might say you do not know what you are talking about Eloy? You are whupped. You might even say, Eloy, I am in charge at my house. I will say to you ok then RAMBO you keep doing what you are doing and see how long you stay married. We need to get back to the basics and enjoy our relationships.

Something I would like to mention is that your children are watching how you treat each other. They will ask themselves is that what I want in a marriage?

To summarize this chapter I will say that she wants a man after God's own heart, with a vision for the future with her and the children. She wants a praying man that prays for wisdom, seeks wise council, and a man that will honor the marriage covenant. That is what she desires. Is that how *The Dash* will be spoken about in your marriage?

CHAPTER 4

The Blessing Of The Tithe

-

Some of you skipped this chapter because it said tithes. "I will read it later," you said, so here you are. I asked God "Why a chapter about the Tithe"? God told me that most people do not give because they do not understand the tithe and how important it is.

I want you to know that I believe in tithing and will tell you my own experiences. Some of you do not believe in tithing and I pray that after you read this chapter your heart will change.

I want you to know when you give according to The Word of God that God will bless the tithe. Have you ever read or heard that God Can Not LIE! That is right, read Hebrews 6:18 when you get a minute.

Some of you look at tithing and say, "It's just the Old Testament, and it's not for now". Let me ask you this, did God say that He would bless Abraham and his seed (heirs)? If you accepted Christ in your life then you are an heir. All the promises for Abraham are for you as well. Not good enough? Let us look at it like this. The Bible says that God loves a cheerful giver in 2 Corinthians 9: 6-7. Take a minute to read it before moving forward.

So many people say things like I only give a little because the preacher uses it wrong. When you give you have to look at your heart. Are you giving with a cheerful heart or are you looking at how it will be used? God wants to bless you but you are not letting Him because you are so worried on how it will be used. Do you know when your blessing starts? When you drop it in the offering bucket or the plate. The blessing does not start when the preacher spends it or how it is distributed. If the church or preacher uses it wrong they have to answer to God. If they answer to me, then I am playing God.

Look at the widow in the book of Mark 12: 41-44 that put in two mites. Compared to today's standards that is less than a penny. But Jesus said that she gave all she had. Her heart was right. This all goes back to having your heart right in your giving. It is not the amount. First, God wants your heart right. If you give with the right heart God says the blessings will come. If you give grudgingly then it is best to not give.

Please understand that tithing is not a get rich quick scheme. It is for your benefit and it does not mean that you will always get money in return. In the book of Malachi 3: 8-12 it says that God will open the windows of heaven and pour out blessings onto your life. If you tithe!

It says that God will bless you so much that you will not

have room to contain it. Again, the blessings could be having a great marriage, your wayward children returning or maybe it could be a financial miracle.

It is important that you pray over your finances. It is important that you stand in agreement with your spouse when writing or giving your tithes. I mentioned earlier that God can not lie and God wants you to remind Him of His Word. It is not that God forgot His Word; it is that God wants you to know what scriptures you are standing on.

I know this is difficult for some of you. But, I want you blessed. I promise you if your heart is right this will work. When it is all said and done did you leave the legacy for your children that you desired? I want you to say this prayer with your spouse the next time you give.

"Jesus, as we give this tithe I will stand on your Word that you will rebuke the enemy. I pray that you open up the windows of heaven and pour out blessings over our lives. Thank you that our marriage is strong and that there is a hedge of protection around our family. I pray that my heart stay right in my giving".

— In Jesus name, Amen.

CHAPTER 5

Telling My Kids About The "S" Word

Some of you skipped straight to this chapter because you are dealing with teaching your kids about sex right now. So here it goes. I want you to know that I believe it is the parent's responsibility to talk to their kids about this important subject. It is not the school counselor, the neighbor, your friends or even the pastor's responsibility to explain it to them.

I was fortunate to be able to explain it to my sons. I also talked to my daughter about some of the things on the boy's side. But, I left the rest up to her mother to explain the female side. More on my daughter later.

Some of you may be wondering how I did this. First, I asked The Lord to give me the right words Second, I knew when it was time. Third, I sat them down and was open to any questions that they might have. I told them that I would be honest and that I did not want them to be embarrassed about sex. I told them that it was from God and that it was a beautiful thing between a husband and wife.

I was talking to one of my son's and I asked him if he knew anything about sex? He said my "friend at school told me all about it." I said, ok, explain it to me. As he started I knew that his friend did not know anything about it. So I stopped him and started explaining it to him. With his eyes bugged out I proceeded and he said "My friend doesn't know, huh dad"? I said, "No he doesn't," and I told my son that if he wants to know anything truthfully about sex to come talk to me. I have always had a great relationship with my kids and the best way has always been to be honest and teach them in a Godly way.

Let me explain what I mean. In today's society clicking your phone here or there you can open sites that you would not open in front of your mother. I have also talked to men about how they maybe have taught their sons. I have heard things like (I bought him a video) or they would say (I just bought him magazines to figure it out). "When I asked why, they responded" with: That is the type of woman he needs to look for.

It is a shame that we cannot be honest with our children and let them know that a wife is a beautiful and valuable person. What a shame when this wife does not fulfil his expectations and he tells his dad thanks but not what I expected.

I promised to tell you about my daughter. As my daughter was getting noticed by boys she was still naïve in some areas of the opposite sex. Some young men were hugging her tightly when they said hello. When I saw this I sat her down and explained what was happening from the guy's perspective. I also explained to her the importance of staying pure for her husband. It was well received because she knew that I wanted nothing but the best for her.

I was talking to a man one day and he said that he tells his sons, "Go get those girls." I asked him, "What do you tell your daughter"? He looked at me and said "What do you mean"? I said you tell your boys that they should go after those girls but what about your baby girl? "He said" No way. I asked him how he thought the father of those girls feels. He is trying to keep his daughters pure just like you are doing with your daughter. I think that he finally understood and he never brought it up again. I believe he was embarrassed.

Please understand that if we do not explain it to our children with love and honesty they will never know what God desires of them. I know that this is a difficult subject. I ask you to pray for God to give you the right words. Remember this, if you do not teach them, chances are that it will be someone that you might not want to teach them.

What better way to leave a legacy that will honor your kid's future spouse and that they can pass on from generation to generation.

CHAPTER 6

Do My Words Heal or Hurt?

*Proverbs 18: 21 says "death and life are
in the power of the tongue and those that
love it will eat its fruit."*

I want to start by saying a few words that we would say when we were children. You could probably finish the saying, it goes like this: "Sticks and stones may break my bones, but words can never hurt me". We have all said this at one time or another in our childhood, but it is not really true. Words do hurt.

We have been around people that will say or have said things like, "I tell it like it is" or, "I am going to put my two cents in". You have to understand that it is just the hurt that they have from not being able to forgive. I am not saying that you should not speak up or give your input. What I am saying is be careful with the words that you use because you just might have the opportunity to eat those words. So make them sweet.

As I was reading the book of Proverbs I would notice over and over about how it would mention people looking like fools and it hit home. You see I was the guy that was always being a fool with my words and hurting my wife and children. I can promise you that *The Dash* I would have left would not have been good.

PROVERBS 29:11:
"A fool vents all his feelings but a
wise man holds them back".

I have been yelled at, cussed at and at one point it was me doing the yelling and cussing. I made a decision many years ago after hearing a pastor teach on the words out of your mouth. He said you know the words that are coming out of your mouth before you say them and so I decided that I was not going to tear people down just so I could look better than them. As I was more careful with the words out of my mouth my wife made several comments throughout our marriage that she was noticing that I was more patient with her and the kids. It was making a difference and I started to see the results as I was becoming more of a teacher with my kids, and was able to explain things without getting all upset.

Please know that as a Christian I am not walking around with a Bible in one hand and anointing oil in the other ready to slap people on the forehead. I still get upset because I am tired from lack of sleep or because of things in my life that might be overwhelming. The words that I speak might be hurtful at times, but I am quick to say that I am sorry and give my family a quick hug after realizing that I hurt them.

I believe that you want to have a beautiful relationship

with your family as well. It starts by you saying things like," I am sorry that I haven't been the best husband, the best dad or the best brother. I will try to change the words that I speak and it will take time so please bear with me". I would like to share a story and we will move on to the last chapter.

I noticed a man that was very hurtful with his words to his wife and children. I finally had an opportunity to sit down with him and I was able to ask him some questions. I started by asking him how his relationship was with his father growing up. He looked at me and said "My dad was mean. My dad would hit me. He would always yell at me so we never had a close relationship". I said," I am not sure if you know this but, you are becoming just like your dad. Don't you want to break the generational curse"? He looked at me with tears in his eyes and said, "It's too late". I said, "It's never too late". "I told him" Go home and sit down in front of your family and ask them to forgive you. Repent, on how you have acted and tell them that you will work on how you talk and that you desire a better relationship with them". He said, "I can't do that, I have too much pride". I said let that pride go or they will leave you as soon as they can and not return. He said, "I just can't". The latest update was that the children are out of the house not wanting to return or have any type of relationship with him.

Can you imagine what *The Dash* he leaves will look like? Remember this: people are watching you.

CHAPTER 7

What Legacy Will You Be Leaving Now?

Some of you thought that legacies are just made on a football or baseball field. I can promise you that you will be leaving a legacy. Better yet what will *The Dash* say about you? At the beginning I had asked you to say a simple prayer to ask God to change your heart to receive these words. Why? Because you know as well as I do that some of the words in this book hit you right between the eyes and other words hit you in the heart. You are the only person that can change you. You can keep blaming dad, mom, Uncle Charlie or Aunt Sue. What you need to say is, "God I do need to change *The Dash* that I was going to leave to be a better more Godly dash".

In the introduction section I asked you some questions, and asked you to give yourself an honest grade as a husband, as a father and as a Man of God. I believe that your family will notice some of those changes for the better.

Just remember that it will take time.

The saying goes that if you want to know what a person is like, you need to ask his wife and children. I am opening myself up here, but I asked my wife and children to give an honest assessment of how I am as a husband and father. I can promise you that I did not bribe them. I did tell them that they would be left out of the will. Just kidding of course. Here is what they had to say.

From my wife Karen, "Eloy gave his life to Jesus about 6 months before we were married. It has been amazing to see how his personal relationship with Jesus and how the Word of God has changed him to the man he is today. His integrity is off the charts and his word means everything to him. It means the world to me to have a husband that seeks God for direction and guidance for our family. It is beautiful to see how God is using him. We have been married for over 32 years and the best is yet to come!"

From my daughter Jessica, "When I think about my dad, there are several words that come to mind that represent his life and the legacy that he has passed down to me over the years. The most significant word that comes to mind is Integrity. Integrity is defined as having the quality of being honest and fair no matter the circumstances. My dad has always been a man of his word and has truly taught me what it means to have Integrity in my own life. His kindness and love exude in everything that he does and no matter what I'm going through in my own life, I can always count on him to be there for support. In the same way that he has lived his life, I strive to live my life too. The legacy that he has built over the years will continue to live from generation to generation".

From my son Nicholas, "My father has taught me many things that have made me the man that I am today. However, I'm not just a man, I am also a brother, a friend, a husband and a father. The thing that every one of these sides of me has learned to do is appreciate the time that I spend with my family and friends. This is a legacy my father's left for me. To make time to spend with the ones you love. You have to go to work, you have to do chores and you have to be an adult, but you choose to be a good son, a good brother, a good friend, a good husband and a good father. In my eyes, my father was all of these things and this is the legacy that my sons will inherit thanks to my dad".

From my son Matthew, "There are many things that my dad has taught me over the years. One of the things that I love the most about him is that he practices what he preaches. There are a few more things that stick out about his life. He has always taught me how my word is my bond and that your word should mean everything. Always being on time, when he said he was going to be somewhere, he is always there. Also, you can achieve many things in life through work ethic and drive. I think a hard work ethic is the basis of integrity which is an integral part of who he is. My dad always told me these things will set you apart from everyone and they will know you by how you handle yourself day in and day out. My dad said when the world hears your last name, your name will define who you are as a man. This life is short so make it right. I would not be who I am without this Man of God".

From my son Joshua, "My dad was and always will be a great example of what a father, husband, and a friend should be. "Pops", as we call him, has always walked what he talked. He made a point in raising us to have a sense of integrity about us. He taught us that our word was worth nothing if we didn't keep it. You never know what your parents are truly going through when you are a child. Looking back on certain things, I hope to have the same kind of patience and God- given wisdom he had during those times. I have so much respect for a man who stays busy at work, takes care of his loved ones, and follows his calling to pilot a men's ministry in his free time. If you're reading this book I hope you are inspired by an author who has had many personal mountains, but looked to God to help him get over them.

You might ask why Eloy had his family type things about him. Well, as I was starting to write this chapter I had asked God how he wanted me to complete the final chapter and that is what God said to do. I believe it is so men can see that we can change. "Eloy changed, so I can change as well". I was honest with the grades that I wrote down at the beginning for me. *The Dash* for Eloy would not have been a good one, I promise.

Prayers

I have a couple of prayers that you might be interested in.

If you were to die today, tomorrow or next year my question to you is, "Where are you going? Heaven or Hell"? This is the most important decision you will ever make because it's Eternal. I would like for you to say a simple prayer with me if you are not sure.

"Jesus, I believe that you died and rose again after the third day. I believe that you died so that I could have Eternal life. Jesus, I ask you to forgive me of my sins and I want to make you the Lord of my life. In Jesus name, Amen".

The other prayer is one that will help you in your marriage. Feel free to print it and put it on the refrigerator.

"LORD,

I thank you for my spouse. I ask for wisdom, favor and direction in every area of our lives. Lord, that you are Honored and Glorified in everything we do. Lord that we look to serve each other before we think of ourselves. I am committed to love my spouse through the ups and downs. Teach me to communicate. Teach me to love them like you would love them.

In Jesus Name, Amen"

Acknowledgements

I am so grateful to so many people in my life that have helped me change and have instilled so many things during this journey.

To my wife, Karen (Purdy). Thank you for your continued support. You have continuously been there for me with prayer and a love that only God can place in a person. Thank you for pushing m e to write this book.

To all my children. "You are so awesome". God wants the best for you and I believe you will achieve it. I love you so much and thank God for each one of you.

To my wonderful daughter-in-laws, Alexandra and Holly. God has blessed this family with you. You make it easy to be a father- in-law. Love you and may God continue to bless you.

To my beautiful grandsons, Oliver, Grayson and Logan. What a blessing you are to the family. "POPS" loves you so much.

To my cousin Joe Cortez for helping design the book cover. You have been so patient with me through it all. You are the best "Cuz".

To Roy Waldrep, Karen Huerta and Joshua Huerta for help in editing the book. God has really blessed you with a talent.

I would also like to thank the Lord for my brothers (Lionel and Guadalupe "aka" Pito) and my sisters (Bertha, Anita and Tina). The support that they have always shown me is incredible. Thank you.

To my brothers and sisters-in-laws. Kevin and Debbie Vincent, Doug and Robin Vincent, Lisa Huerta, Adrian Cadena and Chris Casas. Thank you for always being beautiful people.

To my Mom, (Maria Luisa). Ma, you taught me so much growing up. Even though you have been in heaven for a while you are always in my thoughts. I still remember the talks and the corny jokes that you would laugh at. Love you Ma.

To my in-laws, David and Yvonne Vincent. Dave, after my dad passed away you stepped in and became the father figure in my life. You are a beautiful man of God. Love you and miss your friendship.

About the Author

Eloy Huerta has been married to Karen for over 32 years. They have 4 children and 3 grandsons. Eloy has worked in the chemical plant industry for over 30 years. He is the founder of *Men 4 Jesus in Texas* and has ministered to thousands of men to become better Husbands, Fathers and Men of God. You can find Eloy Huerta on YouTube, Spotify and Apple Podcast.

www.ingramcontent.com/pod-product-compliance
Lightning Source LLC
LaVergne TN
LVHW051206080426
835508LV00021B/2840